ECO ACTION

T0024005

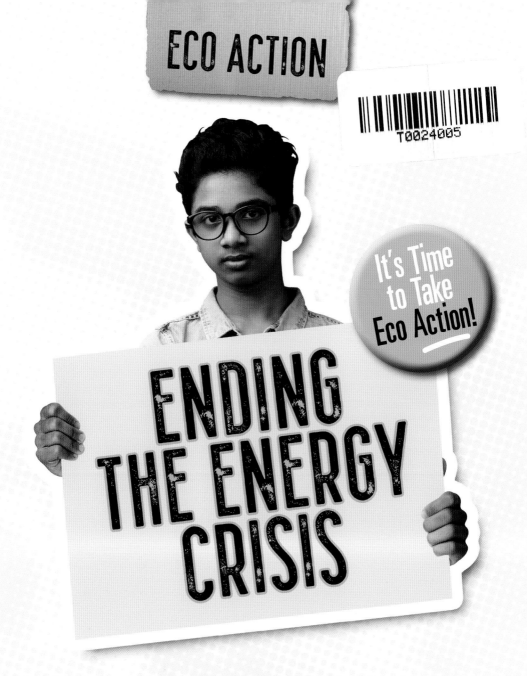

It's Time to Take Eco Action!

ENDING THE ENERGY CRISIS

ROBYN HARDYMAN

CHERITON
CHILDREN'S BOOKS

Published in 2023 by **Cheriton Children's Books**
PO Box 7258, Bridgnorth, Shropshire, WV16 9ET, UK

© 2023 Cheriton Children's Books

First Edition

Author: Robyn Hardyman
Designer: Paul Myerscough
Editor: Jane Brooke
Proofreader: Wendy Scavuzzo
Consultant: David Hawksett, BSc

Picture credits: Cover: Top: Shutterstock/VLADJ55; Center: Shutterstock/
AJP; Bottom: Shutterstock/Juice Verve. Inside: p1: Shutterstock/AJP; pp4-5:
Shutterstock/Mr. James Kelley; p6: Shutterstock/Lukasz Pawel Szczepanski;
p7: Shutterstock/Vadim Petrakov; p8: Shutterstock/Neijia; p9: Shutterstock/
Zstock; p10: Shutterstock/ArtisticPhoto; p11: Shutterstock/Adriana Mahdalova;
p12: Shutterstock/PH888; p13: Shutterstock/CL Shebley; p15: Shutterstock/
Seo Byeong Gon; p16: Shutterstock/Oscity; p17: Shutterstock/Ngel.ac; pp18-19:
Shutterstock/Esbobeldijk; p19: Shutterstock/Vismar UK; p20: Shutterstock/
Andrejs Polivanovs; p21: Shutterstock/Alex Mit; p22: Shutterstock/Terje Aase; p23:
Shutterstock/Petrmalinak; p25: Shutterstock/Brian A Jackson; p26: Shutterstock/
Mopic; p27: Shutterstock/Costazzurra; p28: Shutterstock/Benny Marty; p29:
Shutterstock/Peter Gudella; p30: Shutterstock/Joseph Sohm; p31: Shutterstock/
Stastny_Pavel; p33: Shutterstock/Margaret.Wiktor; p34: Shutterstock/Thomas
Barrat; p35: Shutterstock/Nordroden; p36: Shutterstock/Kletr; p37: Shutterstock/
Rudmer Zwerver; p38: Paul Myerscough; p39: Shutterstock/Fotohunter; p41:
Shutterstock/BigPixel Photo; p42: Shutterstock/Mauro Ujetto; p43: Shutterstock/
Fly_and_Dive; p44: Shutterstock/Elena Elisseeva; p45: Shutterstock/Sergey
Novikov; Throughout: Shutterstock/Voy Ager.

Printed in China

Please visit our website,
www.cheritonchildrensbooks.com
to see more of our high-quality books.

CONTENTS

WHY WE NEED TO TAKE ECO ACTION

Energy powers our world. We use it all the time, in the form of electricity. Electricity enters our homes, schools, and workplaces through cables that come from **power stations**. Gas is burned to heat water that travels through pipes around buildings. The heated water fills radiators, which warm the buildings. Some people also cook using gas. They burn it on the stove. But all this energy use is creating problems for our planet.

Harming the Planet

The way we create energy depends too much on **fossil fuels**. We extract, or take out, coal, oil, and gas from the ground. We burn those fossil fuels to create electricity. That creates gases, such as carbon dioxide (CO_2), which are harmful to our planet. We pump those gases into the **atmosphere**. There, they trap heat and cause changes to our **climate**. Those climate changes harm the natural world, and they threaten us, too. More than half of our energy comes from burning fossil fuels. Scientists tell us it is urgent that we stop doing this. We must find other ways to keep the lights on.

Earth's population is growing—and it is demanding more energy.

A Growing Need

Our huge need for energy is not going to go away. In fact, it is growing. The world's population has doubled in the last 50 years, to about 7.9 billion people. People in wealthy countries have consumed a lot of energy for decades. They continue to consume more and more. But now people in lower-income countries are also demanding more energy. Their economies are growing, and they want to live like people in wealthier countries. They want to heat their homes when it's cold. Many of them live in very hot countries, so they want to cool their homes, too. The processes used to cool homes also use a lot of electricity. This increase in our use of energy is not **sustainable**. Our planet cannot cope with the **pollution** from burning so much fossil fuel.

It's Time to Take Eco Action!

So, what can we do to stop the damage that the energy crisis is causing? We can take action—eco action! Eco action is activity that helps protect the planet. In this book, you'll discover what actions people are taking to tackle the harmful impact of burning fossil fuels. You'll also discover what actions you can take to combat these harmful activities. And you'll learn how you can build a green career that will help protect Earth for future generations. Are you ready to take eco action? Then read on!

CHAPTER 1

ENERGY FROM THE SUN

We are in an energy crisis. But the good news is that there are cleaner ways of producing electricity. They do not create harmful **greenhouse gases** that pollute the planet and cause climate change. These cleaner ways of producing electricity are all around us. They do not run out, which is why they are called renewable energy sources.

Renewable energy sources include the wind, oceans, heat in the ground, and the sun.

Using Energy That Does Not Run Out

Over the past 20 years, people have begun to see the importance of using renewable sources of energy. Some countries have been quicker to develop them than others. In the United States in 2022, around 20 percent of the electricity created came from renewable sources. In the United Kingdom (UK), renewables created around 40 percent of the electricity. There are seven countries that already make almost all of their electricity from renewable sources: Iceland, Paraguay, Costa Rica, Norway, Austria, Brazil, and Denmark.

Using the Sun

The sun is 93 million miles (150 million km) away. Yet, in every hour, enough energy from it reaches Earth to meet the entire world's energy needs for a year! Solar power is created using the energy from the sun. That energy comes in two forms: heat and light. We can use both of them to meet our increasing need for energy.

CLIMATE CHANGE—WHAT'S GOING ON?

The CO_2 that we pump into the air from our power stations is causing a big problem. CO_2 is a greenhouse gas. Greenhouse gases warm the atmosphere. Earth is getting hotter and hotter. That is causing climate patterns to change. Climate change is one of the major threats facing our planet today. We are seeing extreme weather in many parts of the world as a result of climate change. That weather includes **floods** and **droughts**. It also includes **hurricanes** and **wildfires**.

Solar Power in Use

The simplest use of solar power is for heating. In hot countries, a device installed on the roof of a building can concentrate the heat of the sun to heat water for everyday use. The water is stored in tanks, and no electricity is used to heat it. Solar heat can also be used for cooking. Millions of people around the world do not have access to electricity. They cook over wood fires. The smoke from the fires is bad for their health, though. It also pollutes the atmosphere. A solar oven concentrates the heat from the sun to cook the food inside it. It can also boil water. However, the problem with both of these solar-powered devices is that they work only when the sun is shining. For that reason, they work best in hot, sunny places. They cannot be used in cooler places.

Solar ovens are ideal for **remote** hot places where there is no electricity. These solar ovens are in the Himalayas, in Asia.

ELECTRICITY FROM SUNLIGHT

Sunlight is turned into electricity using **solar panels**. The process is called photovoltaics (PV). The panels are made using a material called **silicon**. It can absorb the energy in sunlight and turn it into an electric **current**. We have been using this technology in a small way for decades. For example, small solar-powered batteries are used in calculators and watches. But in the past two decades, the energy industry has found ways to make the technology work for us on an enormous scale.

On the Roof

Solar panels are installed on the roof of a building. To get the most sunlight, they should face the sun. In the northern **hemisphere**, that means facing south. The panels on the roof are connected to a battery. It stores the electricity, so it is available at night. The electricity is transported from the battery and throughout the building through wires. They supply lighting and power points.

Not for Everyone

There are a few challenges with solar power. One is that there must be enough sunlight to create the electricity. The panels do not function well when they get very hot. They actually work better on a cool, but very sunny, day than on a hot, sunny day. On a cloudy day, less electricity will be produced. The supply is therefore not reliable. The second issue is that not all buildings will have a roof area that faces in the right direction. The panels may be in shade for part of the day. That will result in less electricity being produced, too.

A solar panel is made up of many PV cells, like the one shown left.

Long-Term Savings, Short-Term Costs

Installing solar panels is expensive. The technology is quite complex, and the system must be installed to last a long time. The high cost makes it unsuitable for some people. Solar energy has some long-term cost savings, however. People who can afford their own solar electricity take less electricity from the main grid. The grid is a network of energy that serves everyone in the country. People must pay for energy from the grid. In the long term, having your own solar energy supply means that you do not have to pay for as much electricity from the grid. However, it can take several years for that saving to match the cost of installing the solar panels. Fortunately, the cost of installing solar panels has reduced in recent years.

Fitting buildings with solar panels benefits the **environment.** As more people discover that, and solar panels become affordable, more homes will be fitted with them.

FINDING THE SUN

Some buildings are not suitable for solar panels because they do not face the sun. But now there is a solution to that problem. The panels are put on mounts that move. They turn slowly through the day, following the sun. That allows them to capture as much energy as possible.

LITTLE AND LARGE

One of the benefits of solar power is that it can be used in many different ways. Users can start small, with just a single solar panel to provide a small amount of power. Alternatively, they can cover their roofs with enough panels to meet all their electricity needs. Entire fields can be covered with panels, creating a solar power farm. This larger-scale operation can create enough electricity to power a local community. The electricity can also be sent to the main grid, to benefit everyone.

Solar Power Plants

To make a real difference to the way that countries create their electricity, solar needs to be used on a massive scale. That means building solar power stations. The clean electricity they create can be distributed through the grid. That means everyone can benefit from it. Solar power plants need a lot of space. Hundreds or even thousands of panels are laid out across the land, facing toward the sun. They do not produce any pollution, but they do have a visual impact on the environment. That is why the largest power plants are often located in remote areas. In India, the Kamuthi solar park in Tamil Nadu covers 2,500 acres (1,012 ha). Its 2.5 million solar panels supply enough clean energy to power 150,000 households.

This waterfront in the Chinese city of Shanghai is covered in solar panels to provide power to the city.

STORING THE POWER

PV panels can produce electricity only when the sun shines on them. In a sunny place, such as southern California, there are about 5.5 hours of usable sunshine a day. The solution to providing a regular energy supply is to use a battery to store the electricity created from solar power. On sunny days, when more energy is produced than is needed, the battery stores the extra power for future use. The energy industry is working hard on improving the technology of storage batteries. They are the key to making solar power suitable for more people.

Solar panels provide energy to people who live in remote low-income areas. This woman is charging her solar flashlight in the sunlight in Kenya, Africa, so it will be ready to use during the night.

Helping People in Need

One of the great things about solar power is that it can deliver electricity to places where there is no power grid. It can serve remote areas anywhere. It can also serve low-income countries where the electricity grid is patchy. Nearly 20 percent of the world's population has no electricity grid, but solar power is changing that. Having a small area of solar panels can change lives. With electricity, people can keep in touch with each other because they can charge a cell phone. They can stay up after dark, with lights that allow young people to study and improve their education. Having streetlights also makes communities safer.

TAKING ECO ACTION:

SUNSHARE

One organization that is taking action to make it easier for people to benefit from solar power is SunShare. Many people would like to help the planet by switching to a clean, renewable energy source. However, sometimes it is just not possible for them to install solar panels where they live. Perhaps they have no roof space, or they live in an apartment block where solar panels cannot be installed. Perhaps the cost of installing the panels is just too high for them. One person had an idea to help solve those issues.

Sharing the Energy

David Amster-Olszewski was living in Colorado Springs, Colorado, when he had the idea of taking solar power to people in a new way. He started to build "solar gardens." They are small solar power installations in local communities. He called his company SunShare. People can buy a share in their local solar garden. By doing so, they are buying a part of the energy the garden produces. In return, they get a reduced bill from their regular energy **supplier**. This is an affordable way for anyone to enjoy renewable energy.

As people become aware of the benefits of communal solar power, more may choose to invest in a local solar garden to supply their energy needs.

Greenbank Farm Community Solar Garden in Whidbey Island, Washington, is another example of a community-led solar power garden. The garden is part-owned by local residents.

Take It with You

Another big advantage of being part of SunShare is that members can take their membership with them when they move. If you have installed solar panels on your roof, but then moved to a new address, you will lose the benefit of them. If you are in SunShare, you can still be a part of it if you move within the same community. And if you sell your home, you can even choose to sell your SunShare membership with it.

Spreading Success

The idea of community solar power caught on quickly. SunShare soon became a successful company. Recently, it announced plans to expand into new states in the Midwest and Northeast of the United States. More and more people are realizing what a great idea Sunshare is. Other companies have started following Sunshare's example, and demand for a share in this clean, renewable energy is growing.

STARTING SMALL

David Amster-Olszewski started his SunShare business in a small way. He worked alone on the business, from his apartment. He was convinced he had a great idea. And he was right. In the years since it started, SunShare has grown and grown. It has served more than 13,000 customers. That shows that individuals really can make a difference to the problem of the energy crisis.

TAKE ECO ACTION AT SCHOOL

Organizations like SunShare are taking positive action to change the way we create our electricity. And there are positive actions that you can take to help improve our energy crisis, too. You spend a lot of your time at school. Here are some ways you can take action while you're there. By taking eco action, you will be playing an important part in helping to solve our energy issues.

Turn It Off

Almost everybody uses more energy than they actually need. We leave the lights on when we leave a room. We leave appliances switched on. We use hot water to wash our hands when cold water and soap would do the job just fine. At school, you can join with your classmates and start a campaign to improve some of these things. For example, you could ask your teachers to put up signs reminding people to turn off lights when leaving rooms.

Check Where It Comes From

Find out where your school gets its electricity from. Does the supplier use electricity created by burning fossil fuels? Some energy companies now offer only "green" electricity. That is electricity created from renewable sources, such as solar power. The sources do not create greenhouse gases. You could join your school council and suggest that they switch to a clean energy provider. Schools are great places to set an example to the rest of the community.

Do Your Research

Find out how much solar energy is being created in your area. Ask your teachers if you can create a research project. As part of your studies, go out into the local area and see how many buildings have solar panels on them. Are the buildings mostly homes, or businesses? Can you see why some areas are not suitable for solar power? Are there areas that would be suitable? Write up the results of your survey and share them. Why not include them in the school newspaper? It's important to spread the word about the need for more renewable energy in our communities.

Eco Action Wins

By becoming aware of how energy is used in your school, you'll help reduce the amount of fossil fuels we use to create electricity. By raising awareness, you will highlight the issues around our energy crisis. That will encourage more people to make eco-action changes. That will keep harmful gases from entering the air. Those are all big wins for planet Earth!

ECO ACTION!

ENERGY FROM WIND AND WATER

Sunshine is all around us. So are other natural sources that can be used to create electricity. They are wind and water. Almost everywhere in the world, you can feel the wind on your face. It may be a light breeze, or it may be a gale. That movement of the air contains energy. We can use it to create clean electricity. Have you ever stood by the ocean and watched the power of the waves crashing in? There is energy in that water, too. Wind and water power are valuable renewable energy sources. They produce no harmful greenhouse gases. And we can use them to help solve our energy crisis.

An Old Story

We have been using the power of the wind for centuries. Our first ships crossed the oceans powered by the wind in their sails. On land, the large blades of windmills turned in the wind. They moved the parts of the windmill that ground wheat or corn into flour. Other windmills were used to pump water out of the ground. But a few decades ago, scientists began to develop the idea of using the power of the wind to make electricity. Since then, the use of wind power has grown and grown.

Wind **turbines** do not release harmful **emissions** into the atmosphere. They also do not use a lot of other **resources**, such as water.

16

How Does It Work?

To make electricity, wind power is used to turn the blades of large windmills. They are called wind turbines. The turning blades are connected to a turbine inside the structures. That creates electricity that can then be stored or sent straight to the grid.

Problems with Wind Power

Although most places experience some wind most of the time, creating electricity from wind power is not straightforward. You cannot simply find a windy area and build turbines there. The wind must be as regular and reliable as possible. To be effective, a wind turbine needs huge blades. That means it must be very tall. Wind turbines are as tall as 20-story buildings, with blades more than 100 feet (30 m) long.

A single wind turbine will not create a lot of electricity. A lot of turbines are required to create a good supply of electricity. The turbines are therefore built in large groups, creating **wind farms**. They take up a lot of land. They also have a big visual impact on the environment.

Some people do not like the appearance of wind farms. They think they spoil the landscape. That is why wind farms are often located in remote areas.

A GIANT WIND FARM

Wind farms take up a lot of land. One of the world's largest wind farms is the Alta Wind Energy Center in California. It covers 3,200 acres (1,295 ha) in the foothills of the Tehachapi Mountains. The farm includes 586 turbines. The electricity it produces serves more than 250,000 homes.

WIND OUT AT SEA

The energy industry is aware of the difficulty of placing huge wind farms on the land. In countries with few remote areas, wind farms can be an unpopular choice. Fortunately, there is another way to use the clean, green power of the wind to meet our growing energy needs. Wind farms can be located out in the oceans. They are called **offshore** wind farms.

Strong and Steady

The wind usually blows stronger and more steadily out at sea than it does on land. That makes the oceans a great location for wind farms. Offshore wind farms are not as visible to people. The turbines may be seen from the shore, but they are a long way off. They seem to fade into the sky. Energy companies have been developing offshore wind farms in many locations.

Attaching It

There are some obvious challenges to offshore wind. Conditions at sea can be extreme. The equipment used must be tough enough to survive in salty water, big waves, and strong winds. And how do you attach a huge wind turbine to the ocean floor, in deep water? In the early days of offshore wind power, turbines had to be located quite close to the shore, because the water there was not very deep. The technology for attaching turbines to the ocean floor is improving all the time. That allows them to be positioned in deeper water.

A NECESSARY INVESTMENT

It is very expensive to install an offshore wind farm. The high cost is slowly coming down, however. That is because more people are determined to invest in wind farms, and wind farm technology is improving. The cost of not investing in wind farms is also high. That is the cost of increasing climate change problems if we do not clean up our energy supply. Experts agree that offshore wind power has a big role to play in reaching that goal.

Huge power cables carry the electricity from offshore wind farms back to the land.

Floating Farms

The latest development in wind power is floating wind farms. The turbines float in the water. They are held in place by very strong cables connected to the ocean floor. The enormous turbines are built on land. They are then pulled out to sea by ships. The first offshore floating wind farm began operating in 2017. It is located off the coast of Scotland in the UK. Other countries such as the United States, Norway, Portugal, South Korea, and Japan are now installing or planning floating wind farm projects.

This artist's impression shows how the turbines of a floating wind farm are tethered, or attached, to the seabed by long cables.

THE POWER OF WATER

Water covers more than 70 percent of the surface of the Earth. The movement of water contains energy, and that energy can be used to make electricity. However, in the world of renewable energy, power from water has not been greatly used. Water power has huge potential. However, there are big challenges in using it.

Dangerous Oceans

The ocean can be a hostile, or dangerous, place. Out at sea, there are huge waves, frequent storms, and very high winds. Oceans are not easy places in which to install machines. The difficulty and the high costs of water power mean that few people have invested in it. However, there is now an urgent need to explore all the possible options for creating clean energy. For that reason, scientists are researching new ways in which to use water power.

The ocean is full of energy. If we can use just some of it, that could help us solve our energy problems.

ENERGY CLOSE TO HOME

Around two-thirds of people in the world live within 250 miles (402 km) of a sea coast. In the United States, more than half the population lives within 50 miles (80 km) of the coast. It makes sense to create clean electricity close to where all those people live. The cost of transporting it from where it is made to homes and businesses will therefore be lower.

Capturing the Power of the Waves

There are two main ways to use the power of the ocean: wave energy and **tidal** energy. Wave power machines convert, or change, the movement in ocean waves into electricity. The movement of waves is complicated, however. They can move from side to side, and up and down. It is a challenge to design machines to extract the energy from these random movements. Some designs for wave power machines float on the surface. They bounce up and down in the waves. Other designs have long paddles beneath the water. They are attached to the seabed. The paddles are washed back and forth by the ocean's rise and fall.

Using the Power of the Tides

Tidal power uses the slow movement of the ocean toward the shore and out again. That happens twice every 24 hours. It is a regular, **predictable** movement. That makes tidal energy reliable. There are two main ways to use it. The first is with turbines installed in the water. They have blades that turn in the sea current. The movements are used to make electricity. The second way is to build a huge structure called a **tidal barrage**. It is similar to a dam. A **reservoir** fills up with water as the tide comes in, and empties as it goes out. The movement of the water in and out is used to create electricity.

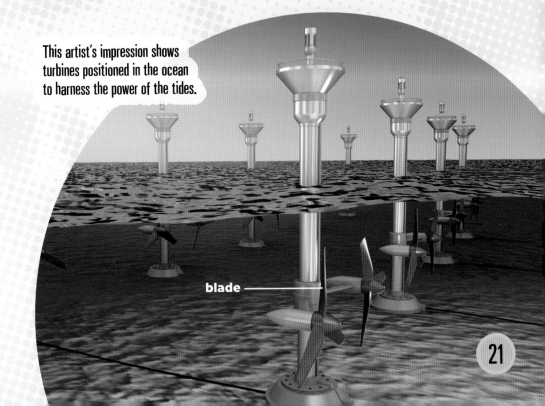

This artist's impression shows turbines positioned in the ocean to harness the power of the tides.

blade

21

TAKING ECO ACTION:

BATWIND

One of the problems with wind power is that the wind does not blow at the same strength all the time. When it is very windy, wind turbines create a lot of electricity. When it is calm, they create much less. That uneven supply does not match the needs of electricity users. They need a reliable supply all the time. The solution to the problem is to store the electricity, so that there is plenty when it is needed. Electricity is stored in batteries. One project that has been developing effective batteries is Batwind.

These Hywind turbines are being transported to the wind farm off the Scottish coast.

How to Store It?

The problem of storing electricity is shared by many renewable sources. They include solar, wind, and water power. They all create an irregular supply. The main electricity grid must have enough power to meet the needs of its customers. That need has made some people unsure about the part renewables can play in solving the energy crisis. It's the biggest issue facing renewable energy companies today. It is a big and very important problem. Batwind is playing an exciting part in solving it.

A SUSTAINABLE FUTURE

The company behind Batwind is called Equinor. It is an energy company that also uses fossil fuels such as oil and gas. Equinor is serious about improving its sustainability. It is committed to developing projects, such as Batwind, that will give renewable energy sources a much bigger role in our energy future.

An Energy Warehouse

Batwind was developed to be used with the first floating offshore wind farm. That is off the coast of Scotland and is called Hywind. It opened in 2017. It creates a lot of electricity, which needs a lot of storage. Batwind is a collection of powerful batteries. They are housed in buildings on the coast near the wind farm. Together, they can hold as much electricity as more than 128,000 smart phones. It's an energy warehouse!

Super Smart

Batwind is also a "smart" system. That is what makes it so special. The system can understand when to store power and when to send it to the grid. The batteries are connected to a computer system. That collects and stores data, or information, about many factors that affect the electricity supply. They include the weather, the time of day, how the main grid is performing, and the needs of energy customers. Batwind uses that data to control the amount of electricity that is either released to the grid or stored for future use. The more data provided, the smarter the system becomes.

Energy created by offshore wind farms can be stored in a collection of large batteries, like the ones shown in this artist's impression.

Projects such as Batwind are taking positive action. They are trying to solve the problems of storing the electricity produced by renewable sources. And there are positive actions that you can take to improve the way you use energy at home, too. By taking eco action, you will be playing an important part in solving our energy crisis.

Check It Out

Check out who is supplying electricity to your home. Is it an energy company that burns fossil fuels to create electricity? If it is, you could ask the people who choose your supplier to think about switching. Choose a company that delivers only electricity from renewable sources. The more people that demand clean energy, the more companies will supply it.

Get a Smart Meter

Most of us do not know how much electricity we use, and how much we waste. A meter in our home measures the units of electricity we use, to figure out the cost. Ask if you can install a smart meter in your home. It monitors the amount of electricity being used. A display shows you the amount and the cost of that electricity. That information can help people control the amount of electricity they use. More than 100 million smart meters have been installed in the United States. They are in about half of all homes. Make sure yours is one!

Switch It Off

Sometimes, the simplest solutions are the most effective. You can save a lot of energy in your home by switching off the power when it is not needed. Turn off lights when you leave a room. Turn off appliances when you're not using them.

Eco Action Wins

By finding out about the amount of electricity you use at home, you will find you can use less of it. You will save money on your electricity bill, and help with the energy crisis at the same time. And if you switch to a renewable electricity supplier, you will reduce the amount of harmful greenhouse gases in the atmosphere. Those are all big wins for planet Earth!

Think First

Before you do the laundry, think! Washing and drying machines use a lot of energy. Could you run fewer loads? Washing at a lower temperature will use less energy, too. Instead of using electricity to power a dryer, put the washing on an clothesline to dry, if you can. Use the natural, renewable sources of sunshine and wind to dry your laundry.

ECO ACTION!

CHAPTER 3

ENERGY FROM THE GROUND

We live on an amazing planet. The land may feel cool to our touch, but deep beneath Earth it is hot. The closer you go toward the core, or Earth's center, the hotter it gets. The heat beneath our feet is called geothermal energy, and it is always there. It can be used as a constant source of power. It is another source of clean, renewable energy to help us fix our energy crisis. Geothermal energy produces no harmful emissions, because no fossil fuels are burned by using it. Geothermal power simply uses the underground heat directly, or it transforms it into electricity. However, like other renewable energy sources, geothermal power comes with some challenges.

Heat All the Time

The outer 10 feet (3 m) of Earth's surface stays at a nearly constant 50–61 degrees Fahrenheit (10–16 °C) throughout the year. The changing seasons affect only the very top of that surface, known as Earth's crust. We can use the heat just below the surface to warm our buildings and heat our water directly.

core

Earth is made up of a series of

A Smart Water System

The machine that extracts heat from underground and brings it into our homes is called a ground source heat pump. The device is connected to a series of pipes that are buried underground. The pump circulates a fluid, often water, through the pipes. Down below, the water is heated by the ground. As it returns to the building, that hot water is then used to heat the building. After use, the cooled water is returned to the ground, and the process of heating it begins again. That is a clean alternative to heating buildings by burning gas in a central heating system.

The Issues with Ground Source

One of the problems with ground source heat pumps is the cost of installing them. The heat pumps are not very expensive, but installing the pipes underground can be. A large, deep hole must be dug outside the building. That can be difficult in built-up areas, where there are many nearby buildings. However, once the pipes have been installed and the hole has been filled in, the system should work for decades without any issues.

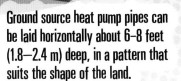

Ground source heat pump pipes can be laid horizontally about 6–8 feet (1.8—2.4 m) deep, in a pattern that suits the shape of the land.

ECO-WIN SYSTEM

A geothermal heat pump system can also be used to cool a building in a hot location. It works when the temperature of the air is hotter than the temperature below ground. The water in the pipes is heated in the air. It is then cooled as it passes underground. It comes out of the ground cooler, to cool the building. Geothermal can provide both heating and cooling with just one system. That's a great eco win!

DEEP UNDER THE EARTH

Ground source heat pumps are great for creating heating on quite a small scale. Each one can serve a building, such as an apartment block, house, or office. However, there is another way to use geothermal energy to solve our energy crisis. And it is a large-scale way. It is to use the heat underground to generate electricity. That is done in a power plant. As a result, a lot of people can benefit from clean, renewable electricity without needing to install a ground source heat pump.

Deep Under the Ground

In some places beneath the surface, hot water is found. It can be as hot as 200 degrees Fahrenheit (93 °C), or more. Geothermal power plants have been set up around some of those places. Sometimes, hot water reaches Earth's surface. The result is a geyser, or hot spring. There are great examples of geysers at Yellowstone National Park, in California. The geysers cannot be used for geothermal energy, however. That is because the park is protected.

Hot water explodes spectacularly from geysers in Yellowstone National Park.

LEADING THE WAY

Some countries are using a lot of geothermal energy. Kenya in Africa creates about half of all its electricity in geothermal power plants. Indonesia, the Philippines, Turkey, and Iceland have also developed a lot of geothermal energy. The world leader in geothermal energy is the United States. The west of the country has perfect conditions for drilling, because it is near the Pacific Ring of Fire. That is an area of great volcanic activity, resulting in a lot of underground heat near Earth's surface. The geothermal electricity produced in California, Nevada, Utah, Hawaii, Oregon, Idaho, and New Mexico is enough to power about 3.5 million homes.

This power plant is in Iceland, a country with a lot of geothermal power.

Superhot Water

To tap into geothermal energy, a deep well is drilled down into the ground until it reaches an area of hot water. The well allows steam to **erupt** from the ground. The steam is then used to power a turbine that creates electricity. A different design of power plant is used where there is no hot water underground. At this type of plant, two wells are drilled. Cool water is piped into the ground through one well. The water is then heated by heat in the ground. The heated water is then brought back up to the surface through the second well. At the surface, the water becomes superheated and turns into steam. That steam is used to power turbines.

A Heavy Cost

The main disadvantage of geothermal energy as a source of electricity is its cost. It is very expensive to drill far beneath Earth's surface. That has stopped some energy companies from developing geothermal energy.

TAKING ECO ACTION:

ALTAROCK ENERGY

One company that is trying to make geothermal energy easier to produce is AltaRock Energy. This American company was started by an **engineer** named Susan Petty. She wanted to see if she could make it easier to use the heat deep down in the ground for electricity.

No Pools? No Problem!

One problem with geothermal energy is that the reservoirs of hot water underground do not naturally occur in many places. In the United States, for example, they are far more common in western areas than elsewhere in the country. Susan Petty and AltaRock have invented a process that does not need an underground water reservoir. It is known as an Enhanced Geothermal System (EGS). It involves pumping water into the ground into cracks that naturally occur 2–3 miles (3.2–4.8 km) below the surface. First, the water slightly opens the cracks. Then, water pools, creating a new reservoir of water.

Geothermal power plants can produce a constant supply of electricity. It is more reliable than wind or solar energy.

A lot of food is grown all year around in these glasshouses in Iceland, which are heated and lit using geothermal power. Iceland is fortunate because it has plenty of geothermal power. However, EGS systems could make similar sustainable projects possible almost anywhere.

Nothing Wasted

The natural heat of the ground heats water in the reservoir to around 600 degrees Fahrenheit (316 °C). The hot water and the steam that is also created are then pumped back to the power plant on the surface. There, the steam is used to turn turbines that produce electricity. When the used hot water has cooled, it is sent back underground to start the process all over again. The water is not wasted.

Fixing the Future

Susan Petty studied geology at university. She started her company AltaRock in 2017. Since then, she has grown the business and raised millions of dollars for research and development projects. The people at AltaRock are looking across the United States for new locations for geothermal power plants. Their exciting new technology could make geothermal power possible in many more places. It also makes geothermal energy less expensive to develop. That may mean geothermal could join wind and solar power as a major contributor to the world of renewable, sustainable energy.

A PERFECT PROBLEM SOLVER

The beauty of this EGS system is that it can be used almost anywhere where water can be pumped into the rock. There is no need for an underground area of hot water to already exist. EGS systems can even be used at existing geothermal power plants. EGS systems can make the existing water areas there bigger. That makes them more productive.

TAKE ECO ACTION
IN YOUR FREE TIME

Companies like AltaRock are taking positive action to make geothermal power possible in more places. And there are positive actions that you can take to help tackle our energy problems, too. By taking eco actions, you'll be helping the planet and the people, plants, and animals that live on it.

Have Green Fun

Think about the energy that is used by the activities you do for fun. Playing on consoles and watching television both use electricity. That electricity had to be made. Perhaps fossil fuels were burned to make it. Try choosing activities that require no electricity. You could go for a walk or a bike ride. You could play sports with friends. Those activities are healthy for you. And by using less electricity, you'll be helping the planet.

Take a Green Vacation

Try to choose vacations that have the least impact on the environment. When you go on vacation, try to leave the car at home if you can. Choose a place that's not too far from where you live. Don't take a plane flight if you can avoid it. Planes and cars burn fossil fuels that contribute to the energy crisis. How about a camping trip? You can enjoy a beautiful landscape without harming it or creating pollution. Take bicycles or rent them when you arrive. That way, you can explore without using any energy at all—except your own, of course!

Turn It Down

Winter vacations at home can be cold. It's tempting to turn up the heat to keep warm, but try not to. If you turn the heat down by just one degree, you will save a lot of energy. Your energy bill will be lower, too. Put on another sweater to keep warm, or get some exercise to keep warm instead.

Eco Action Wins

By thinking about the energy you use in your leisure activities, you can help change the way we create it. Just by getting more creative in your choices, such as choosing physical activities over watching television or playing on consoles, you can make changes that help reduce climate change. They will be big eco wins for planet Earth—and for you!

ECO ACTION!

CHAPTER 4

OTHER SOURCES OF ENERGY

As the demand for energy around the world is increasing so fast, we need to find more ways to create energy. Renewable sources such as solar, wind, and geothermal energy can all be part of that plan. But none of them can solve the problem on their own. We need them all. And we need some more ideas, too.

Nuclear Energy

There is one source of energy we have been using for more than 60 years. That is nuclear energy. It contributes around 11 percent of the world's electricity. Nuclear energy is cleaner than using fossil fuels to make electricity, and it is sustainable. It is also reliable. It can provide a constant supply of electricity. It is not a renewable energy source, however. That is because there is a limited supply of the materials needed to create it. But we have enough to last for about another 100 years using current technology, and new sources of **uranium** are also being found.

The St. Lucie Nuclear Plant in Florida has been powering more than 1 million homes for the last 45 years. Could power stations such as this provide power to many more homes in the future?

The activity in modern nuclear power stations is carefully monitored within control rooms.

NEW NUCLEAR

There have been some serious accidents at nuclear power plants in recent decades. The accidents have made some people reluctant to develop nuclear power. They think it is too dangerous. However, our need for more clean electricity is now so urgent that people are looking at nuclear power again. New designs for power plants have also made the industry more effective and safer.

How Does It Work?

Nuclear energy uses the power that exists inside atoms. Atoms are the tiny particles, or pieces, that everything is made of. A lot of heat energy is released when the atoms of a metal called uranium are split apart. That energy releases other tiny particles, which crash into more uranium atoms. That causes more splitting. The process keeps going in a constant stream. The heat the process creates can be used to heat water, which then becomes steam. That steam powers turbines that create electricity.

Problems with Nuclear

Nuclear energy does not release many harmful emissions that add to **global warming**. However, it does have some problems. First, building a nuclear power plant is very expensive. Second, safety is a problem. Harmful energy and particles called **radiation** are released when creating nuclear power. It has to be very carefully controlled. It can cause serious diseases to living things if it escapes into the air or water. Third, the process produces dangerous waste that emits, or gives off, radiation. The waste remains harmful for thousands of years. It has to be buried deeply and securely. That uses a lot of energy and is expensive.

ENERGY FROM NATURE

There are natural substances that can be used to create energy. As we search for more sources of energy, using those substances is becoming more common. The substances are known as **biomass**. Biomass can be made from any material that comes from plants or animals. Two of the biggest biomass energy sources used today are wood and waste. Both can play a part in solving the energy crisis.

Animal waste can be turned into energy at biomass plants.

Energy from Plants and Animals

Biomass materials contain energy that has come from the sun. Plants store the sun's energy in their roots, stems, and leaves when they use sunlight to grow. That energy is passed on to animals that eat the plants. The energy can be released from both plants and animals. It is called biomass energy. We release the energy stored in biomass by burning it. The heat energy it creates can be used directly, to heat water or buildings. It can also be used to create electricity in a power plant.

From Waste to Energy

In countries where there are a lot of forests, wood is an important biomass energy source. When trees are cut down, mainly the trunk is used for wood. A lot of branches and small pieces are left over. When the trunks are cut into planks, more waste wood is created. All that waste can be used. It is collected and burned to create heat. That heat is used in some farming practices, such as heating greenhouses. It can also be made into small pellets. The pellets are sold as fuel.

Garbage Made Green

Our garbage is a biomass energy source, too. It can be collected in huge containers. When air is removed from the containers, the waste breaks down. In that process, a gas called methane is produced. It can be burned to create electricity for local people. The broken-down garbage is also used as a **fertilizer** that helps crops grow.

Cow manure is turned into energy at this biomass power plant.

A BALANCING ACT

There is a big problem with biomass energy. Burning biomass releases CO_2 into the atmosphere. It is a harmful greenhouse gas that is contributing to climate change. However, plants are also very useful at storing CO_2. Through their lives, they soak it up from the air. Some people say that cancels out the pollution created by burning them. Others say we should not add any CO_2 to the atmosphere. We should simply leave plants to be useful carbon storage.

TAKING ECO ACTION:

PLANT-E

Although we face big challenges ahead in our need to solve our energy crisis, there are signs of hope. And some come in the form of smart companies. They include one in the Netherlands in Europe, called Plant-e. The people in this company are working hard to produce electricity from some of the most plentiful things on the planet—plants. That really is green energy!

How Does It Work?

As plants grow, they use the energy in sunlight and carbon dioxide (CO_2) from the air to produce **organic** matter. They use some of that to make themselves grow. The rest of the matter passes into the soil through the plants' roots. The soil is full of tiny **bacteria**. They break down the organic material. When they do that, they produce energy in the form of electrons, which can be used to create electricity! One university student in the Netherlands, Marjorlein Helder, studied that energy. She wanted to find a way to collect and use it. Marjorlein was passionate about finding sustainable energy sources for our future. So she set up her company, Plant-e.

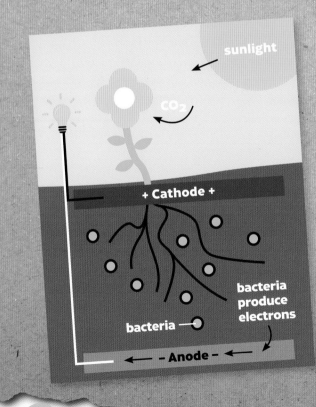

sunlight

CO_2

+ Cathode +

bacteria produce electrons

bacteria

← - Anode - ←

To capture the energy produced by plants, the scientists at Plant-e added an anode and cathode to soil. They are the positive and negative ends of a battery. They were connected to a circuit. Some of the electrons in the soil were then captured and turned into electricity, just like in a battery.

Plants to the Rescue

Plant-e has created a type of battery that collects and stores the electricity plants produce. The electricity is then used to power items such as lights. One plant produces just a small amount of electricity. But, when you consider how many plants there are in the world, you can see the potential of plant electricity. If used on a big scale, it could help solve our energy issues.

Imagine a world powered by plants! The scientists at Plant-e believe that could be one of the keys to helping us produce sustainable energy.

LOTS OF WINS

CO_2 is a big contributor to the problem of global warming and climate change. Growing plants to create electricity also helps reduce the amount of CO_2 in the air. That is because plants take in carbon dioxide from the air. Using plant electricity also does not harm the plants or create any harmful greenhouse gas emissions. Plant electricity is clearly a big eco win for people and the planet!

TAKE ECO ACTION AT WORK

The scientists at Plant-e are taking positive action to find new clean ways to create electricity. And there are positive actions that you can take to help change how we use energy in the workplace. By taking these eco actions, you'll be helping to clean up the atmosphere. That will mean a better, brighter future for our planet and its people.

Ask Adults

Most people spend a lot of time in their workplace. Talk to the adults in your life. Tell them about your concerns about energy and climate change. Ask them to help, for example, they could ask the people who run their workplaces to make better choices about energy. They could suggest that they install solar panels or a ground source heat pump.
If more people ask for eco-friendly energy solutions in their workplaces, more solutions will be found.

Say "Switch Off!"

Too many offices and other places of work blaze with light after dark. When the workers have gone home, the lights are still on. That wastes a lot of energy. And it's not necessary. If you see that happening, you and your friends could write to the people in the building. Ask them to act. If they switch off the lights at night, people in other buildings may follow.

Speak Up!

Make your voice heard! Write to the owners of large businesses. They will own or rent many buildings in which energy use may not be efficient. Ask them to review the energy that their businesses use, and make it greener. Tell them that they have a responsibility to their employees, and your generation, to make green changes that will benefit everyone.

Eco Action Wins

By asking others to think carefully about energy use, you will raise awareness of the issue. That will lead to more people making positive changes that will benefit the planet. If you can persuade big business owners to make changes, the impact could be huge. Even little changes among smaller businesses can help. We all have a duty to change how we work and live. Those changes will result in eco wins for planet Earth, and all of us!

ECO ACTION!

A CLEANER FUTURE FOR ENERGY

There is no doubt that the world is waking up to the problem of the energy crisis. Governments, businesses, and ordinary people all now understand that change must happen. There are signs that the change is beginning to speed up. But there is still a lot of work for all of us to do.

Many young people believe we need to take more eco action, and faster, to protect Earth.

A Start, but Not Enough?

In 2021 leaders, scientists, and campaigners from all over the world came together. They met in the city of Glasgow, Scotland, for an important meeting called COP26. They wanted to agree on plans to reduce our use of fossil fuels—plans that every country would stick to. The agreement they signed took important steps forward. But there is still a huge amount to do. More than 40 countries agreed to stop using coal-fired power stations over the next 10 to 20 years. Some of the biggest coal-burning countries did not sign the deal, however. They include China, India, and the United States. That is a huge problem. The scientists say that even the deal that was agreed on is not good enough. Everyone needs to do more.

Solar thermal power stations are one of the smart solutions that scientists have developed to help solve our energy problems. Solar thermal power stations use mirrors that focus the sun's rays onto a collection tower. The sun's heat energy is collected in the tower, then used to heat water to create steam energy.

collection tower

Catching the Carbon

While we still burn fossil fuels to create electricity, we must find ways to stop the CO_2 the process creates from entering the atmosphere. That process is called carbon capture. It will be an important part of reducing CO_2 in the atmosphere in the next decade. During carbon capture, CO_2 is captured at power plants before it enters the air. It is then safely stored. Several countries, including the United States, have large carbon capture projects underway. Many more are needed around the world. As long as we continue to burn fossil fuels, we must capture its harmful carbon.

Smart New Ideas

New ideas are being developed for the renewable energy sources we use, too. Solar power can be created from thin panels attached to the fronts of buildings. Soon, even the glass in windows will be able to capture solar power. Entire buildings will be able to create their own power on every surface. Some countries do not have an electricity grid. There, solar power panels provide people with clean energy. Solar energy is working on a huge scale, too. Solar thermal power stations have been built in some deserts. They use the heat of the sun, not its light, to create energy. That heat boils water, to create steam that drives turbines.

A Brighter Energy Future

Families, businesses, and governments now understand that we need to make change happen for good. We are all beginning to change our behaviors. And we have better technology than ever before to help us make those changes. If we all take eco action now, and invest in smart science and sustainable living, together we can solve our energy crisis.

BUILD A CAREER IN
ECO ACTION

Why not take more eco action, and develop a career in cleaning up our energy? There are many different career paths that you can explore. Renewable energy is one of the fastest-growing areas of employment around the world today. That is because more and more companies can see how very important it is. And more and more people want to change the way they get and use their energy. The future is exciting, with many new ideas in development. Maybe you will join in that work one day. Your ideas could be part of the solution to our energy crisis. Here are just some of the jobs you could explore.

Help with Solar Power

One of the fastest-growing jobs in the United States today is installing solar panels. Why not learn how to install this exciting technology on people's homes and places of work? You will be transforming their energy use. You will need to be good at practical tasks for this role, and to understand the techniques as they are taught to you. Studying subjects at school and college such as math and engineering will help you get into this career.

Working in the green energy field will help protect Earth.

Get into Science

The new ideas for our energy future will come from scientists. They will discover how to create cleaner electricity. Their research will provide solutions to our energy crisis. You will need a real passion for science to be a research scientist. Studying subjects at school and college such as math, physics, chemistry, and engineering will help you get into energy science.

Spread the Word

Perhaps your skills are in communication. The world needs people who are passionate about fixing the energy crisis. If you love writing about things that matter to you, you could train as a journalist. You can write for national or local newspapers and magazines. You can start your own website and write blogs for your followers. Studying subjects at school such as English, information technology (IT), and social science are helpful for careers in journalism.

Get into Politics

If you want to change policy decisions on eco issues such as energy, why not become a change-maker? Be one of the people making the decisions. You can represent the people in your local district. Maybe one day you will represent your state. Most people working in politics started in their local area. Join your local party, or a group wanting to make the same changes as you. Learn how to organize a campaign. Small campaigns can lead to bigger ones! Studying subjects at school such as English, history, social science, and math will help you find jobs in politics.

The world is going to need more scientists who can figure out great solutions to our ongoing energy crisis. Maybe you could be one of them!

GLOSSARY

atmosphere the layer of gases that surrounds Earth

bacteria very simple living organisms

biomass plant material or animal waste used as a fuel source

climate the regular weather conditions of an area

current electric charges that flow from one place to another in a circuit

droughts periods of time with little or no rain

emissions substances discharged into the air by something, such as machinery

engineer a person whose work is to design and make things that solve problems, such as machines

environment a natural place that surrounds plants and animals

erupt break out of Earth's surface

fertilizer a substance that helps plants grow quicker and bigger

floods the movement of large amounts of water over land that is normally dry

fossil fuels fuels such as coal, oil, and gas that were made from animals and plants that died long ago

global warming an increase in Earth's temperatures, caused by human actions

greenhouse gases harmful gases such as carbon dioxide that collect in Earth's atmosphere and trap the heat of the sun

hemisphere one of the two halves of the Earth, the northern or southern hemisphere

hurricanes powerful storms with heavy rain and strong winds

offshore in the ocean

organic relating to living matter

pollution harmful substances in the air, land, or water

power stations places where electricity is created, collected, and distributed

predictable can be relied upon to happen

radiation a harmful form of energy and particles created in a nuclear power plant

remote far away from towns and cities

reservoir a large pool of collected water

resources materials or supplies that can be used to make something

silicon an element that can conduct electricity

solar panels panels made of substances that collect the energy in sunlight to turn it into electricity

supplier person or organization that supplies goods or materials

sustainable can be relied on for the foreseeable future

tidal related to the tides, the movement of the oceans toward the shore and out again

tidal barrage a huge device to collect the energy in the moving tides of the ocean

turbines machines used to convert the movement of air or a liquid into electricity

uranium a metal used in nuclear power stations to create electricity

wildfires large fires that spread quickly through natural areas

wind farms collections of many wind turbines in one location

FIND OUT MORE

Books

Bard, Mariel. *Geothermal Energy: Harnessing the Power of Earth's Heat* (Powered Up! A STEM Approach to Energy Sources). New York, NY: PowerKids Press, 2018.

Brearley, Laurie. *Water Power: Energy from Rivers, Waves, and Tides* (A True Book: Alternative Energy). New York, NY: Scholastic Children's Press, 2018.

Dickmann, Nancy. *Using Renewable Energy* (Putting the Planet First). New York, NY: Crabtree Publishing Company, 2018.

Hardyman, Robyn. *Solar Power* (Energy Evolutions). Bridgnorth, UK: Cheriton Children's Books, 2022.

Websites

Find out more about an organization taking action on our climate emergency at:
www.acespace.org

Find out about different types of renewable energy and innovations at:
www.alliantenergykids.com

Find out about different types of renewable energy at:
www.eia.gov/energyexplained/index.php?page=renewable_home

Learn more about wind energy at:
www.eia.gov/energyexplained/index.php?page=wind_home

Find out lots more about green careers at:
www.environmentalscience.org/careers

Publisher's note to educators and parents:
All the websites featured above have been carefully reviewed to ensure that they are suitable for students. However, many websites change often, and we cannot guarantee that a site's future contents will continue to meet our high standards of educational value. Please be advised that students should be closely monitored whenever they access the Internet.

INDEX

About the Author

Robyn Hardyman has written many books for children that look at the problems that affect our planet today. In writing this book, she has learned how important it is that we all take eco action and make the changes needed to end the energy crisis and help clean up our planet.